ARMIES OF THE PAST

GOING TO WAR IN
WORLD
WAR I

ARMIES OF THE PAST

GOING TO WAR IN WORLD WAR I

ADRIAN GILBERT

FRANKLIN WATTS

A Division of Scholastic Inc.

NEW YORK TORONTO LONDON AUCKLAND SYDNEY
MEXICO CITY NEW DELHI HONG KONG
DANBURY, CONNECTICUT

🎭 ILLUSTRATIONS BY

Mark Bergin
Kevin Maddison
Lee Montgomery
Steve Noon
Peter Visscher
Maps by Stefan Chabluk

Editor Penny Clarke
Editor-in-Chief John C. Miles
Designer Steve Prosser
Art Director Jonathan Hair
Picture Research Susan Mennell

First published in 2001 by
Franklin Watts
96 Leonard Street
London
EC2A 4XD

First American edition 2001 by Franklin Watts
A Division of Scholastic Inc.
90 Sherman Turnpike
Danbury, CT 06816

Catalog details are available from the Library of
Congress Cataloging-in-Publication Data

ISBN   0-531-14595-6 (lib. bdg.)

CONTENTS

The Road to War

In 1914, Europe was divided into two warring groups of countries. Germany and Austria-Hungary were called the Central Powers. They were opposed by the Allies: Russia, France, Britain, and Belgium.

The leaders of the Central Powers believed that war would break out eventually, and that it would be better for them if it happened quickly. They began to look for a reason to go to war. This reason turned out to be the assassination (killing) of Austrian archduke Franz Ferdinand by Serbian people in Sarajevo.

When Austria-Hungary demanded Serbia's surrender, Russia said it would come to Serbia's aid. The rest of Russia's allies followed, and war was on its way.

The assassination of Archduke Franz Ferdinand
Relations between Serbia and Austria-Hungary were already bad, and this incident led to the outbreak of war.

PORTUGAL

WORLD MAP 1917

Canada
Britain
Russia
Pacific Ocean
United States
Atlantic Ocean
Japan
Togoland
AFRICA
Dutch East Indies
India
New Guinea
Cameroon
German East Africa
New Zealand
German Southwest Africa
Australia

ATLANTIC OCEAN

- Allied Powers
- Central Powers

WORLD WAR I YEAR BY YEAR

The war begins, 1914
The Central Powers declare war against Russia and France. Germany marches through Belgium to attack France, and Britain joins the Allies.

The war develops, 1915
A trench system extends across western Europe. Germany uses poison gas against the Allies. The Russians are pushed back by a major German offensive (attack). Allies fail against the Turks at Gallipoli.

Western Front, 1916
A German offensive against the French at Verdun is stopped at great cost. An Allied offensive along the Somme River also causes many deaths but does not produce a victory for either side.

NORWAY

SWEDEN

Jutland

DENMARK

NETHERLANDS

GREAT BRITAIN

GERMANY

RUSSIA

Ypres

IUM

Somme

Verdun

SWITZERLAND

AUSTRO-HUNGARIAN EMPIRE

FRANCE

ITALY

ROMANIA

BLACK SEA

MONTENEGRO

SERBIA

BULGARIA

SPAIN

CORSICA

Gallipoli

SARDINIA

GREECE

TURKEY

ALBANIA

The Treaty of Versailles

Signed in 1919, the Treaty of Versailles brought the war to a formal close.

The Central Powers of Germany and Austria-Hungary were forced to admit defeat; Germany lost territory, while the Austro-Hungarian Empire was taken apart.

Germany also had to pay reparations (money) to the Allies.

MAP OF EUROPE 1914

MEDITERRANEAN SEA

■ Allied Powers	■ Central Powers	⋯⋯ Western front line of trenches 1914	⚔ Major battle sites
■ Countries joining Allied Powers	■ Countries joining Central Powers	■ Neutral Powers	⛵ Sea battle of Jutland

The naval war, 1916–17

British and German fleets fight at Jutland. Neither side wins, and the Germans are unable to break the British naval blockade of their ports. The Germans use submarines to attack British ships.

Year of decision, 1917

The United States enters the war on the Allied side. Once American armies are trained and ready, Germany is outnumbered. The Russian army begins to collapse as revolution topples the czar.

Defeat of Central Powers, 1918

American troops and equipment help the Allies defeat the Germans on the Western Front. The Germans ask for peace talks in November. By this time, Austria-Hungary and Turkey have already collapsed.

Off to the Front

Once war had been declared, the young men of each nation were "called up," or mobilized, by the army.

In most nations, males aged eighteen and over had to serve up to two years in the army. Each nation could then call upon men who had been given some military training. These men were called conscripts, and during August 1914, they were sent into battle as quickly as possible.

Germany, for example, had a peacetime army of 870,000 regular soldiers. In 1914, it could mobilize a total of 4.3 million soldiers.

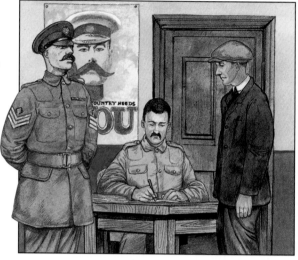

RECRUITING CIVILIANS
Many men who were not conscripts volunteered to fight for their country. Britain relied heavily on volunteers. In 1914, hundreds of thousands of men were recruited into the army.

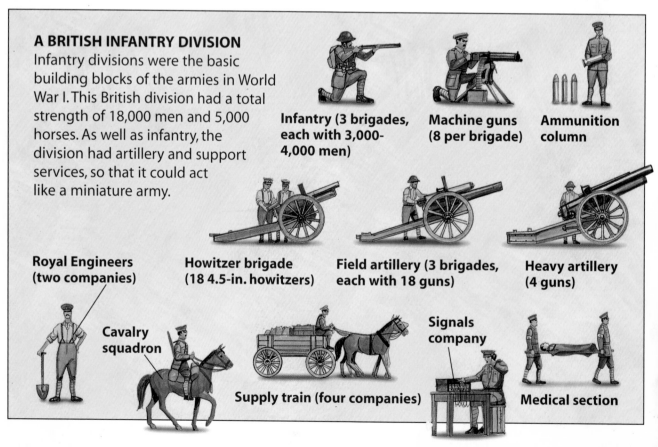

A BRITISH INFANTRY DIVISION
Infantry divisions were the basic building blocks of the armies in World War I. This British division had a total strength of 18,000 men and 5,000 horses. As well as infantry, the division had artillery and support services, so that it could act like a miniature army.

Infantry (3 brigades, each with 3,000-4,000 men)

Machine guns (8 per brigade)

Ammunition column

Royal Engineers (two companies)

Howitzer brigade (18 4.5-in. howitzers)

Field artillery (3 brigades, each with 18 guns)

Heavy artillery (4 guns)

Cavalry squadron

Supply train (four companies)

Signals company

Medical section

EUROPE'S ARMIES

GERMANY
The German army was the best organized in Europe and had highly trained officers who directed the movements of troops. In 1914, Germany mobilized 87 divisions, organized into 8 separate armies.

BELGIUM
The Belgian army was one of the smallest in Europe, with just 117,000 men. Invaded by Germany in 1914, the Belgians could not stop the Germans from conquering most of their country. Still, their army continued to fight with the Allies until 1918.

FRANCE
In the month of August 1914, France mobilized two million men. The French army was determined to attack the Germans any time they could.

💀 OVER BY CHRISTMAS?
Few people had any idea what war would be like. Most soldiers thought it would consist of a few enormous battles that would decide victory. People started saying, "the war will be over by Christmas!" They were to be proved very wrong.

> "It is normal all over the world with young fellows who see war as an adventure. We believed God was on our side. We felt we were defending ourselves, and I was very anxious to be a patriot and help defend my country."
>
> — Carl von Clemm, a German recruit, explaining his emotions on hearing of the outbreak of war

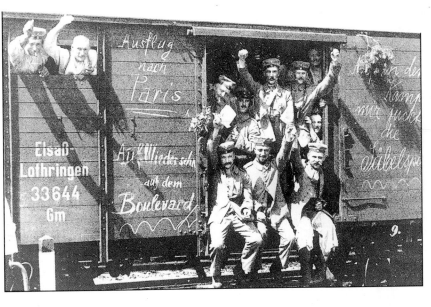

German troops wave from a boxcar as they leave for the front in 1914.

💀 STREAMING TO THE FRONT
The generals on all sides wanted their troops to be transported to the battlefield as quickly as possible. In order to invade France and Belgium, the Germans built thirteen separate railway lines to carry their troops to the border. The French used seven thousand trains to take their forces to the front line in August 1914.

The Western Front

In 1914, Germany sent seven armies to fight the French and British in the west. Only a single army was left to tackle the Russians in the east.

The German plan required four armies to march through Belgium and northern France, surround the main French force, and capture Paris. The plan nearly worked, but the French stopped the Germans at the Battle of the Marne in September 1914.

By the end of the year, fighting battles on open ground had ended. Next were the trenches.

🕷 PROFESSIONAL SOLDIERS

Unlike the huge European armies which were made up of conscripts, the British army was a small force made up of mostly volunteers.

The British were only able to send 150,000 men to France in August 1914, but they played a major role in stopping the German attack. The British realized they would need many more soldiers, so they launched a major recruitment drive.

🕷 UNIFORMS

Infantry are the foot soldiers of the army. British infantry wore khaki uniforms, which helped camouflage (hide) them from the enemy. In 1914, the French still wore blue coats and bright red trousers, which made them easy targets. In 1915, they adopted a blue-gray uniform.

Infantry cap

BRITISH SOLDIER, 1914

Tunic

Ammunition pouch

Lee Enfield .303-caliber rifle

Haversack

Entrenching tool for digging

"Puttees" (leg wraps)

Leather boots

SOLDIERS' GEAR

British steel helmet

German "pickelhaube" helmet

A SOLDIER'S KIT
As every soldier had to fight for several days without receiving extra supplies, he had to carry a lot of equipment with him: a heavy coat or blanket, food and water, and lots of ammunition for his rifle.

Entrenching tool

Bayonet

Ammunition

German Mauser rifle

HELMETS
Shell splinters caused many head wounds. As a result, protective steel helmets were introduced in 1915–16. The British steel helmet came into service in 1916. The German spiked "pickelhaube" helmet — made of leather — was replaced by the "coal-scuttle" steel helmet.

GERMAN INFANTRY GEAR

Shoulder straps

Heavy coat

Blanket

Back-pack

Bayonet

Food bag

Water bottle

Entrenching tool

WEAPONS AND TOOLS
The main weapon of all infantry was a bolt-action rifle, which had a magazine containing five or ten cartridges. A well-trained soldier could fire up to fifteen shots per minute.

For stabbing at the enemy in close combat, soldiers had bayonets on the end of their rifles.

🙂 DEFENSIVE FIREPOWER
Artillery, rifles, and machine guns proved so effective that soldiers were too exposed above ground. As a result, they were forced to dig trenches to survive.

For most of the war, troops in their trenches could always defeat those attacking them across open ground.

🙂 FIELD ARTILLERY
The most dangerous weapon on the 1914 battlefield was field artillery — guns light enough to be moved easily and capable of a very high rate of fire.

The best field gun of the war was the French 75mm gun. This fired up to 20 rounds per minute — one shell every 3 seconds.

FRENCH 75mm GUN AND CREW

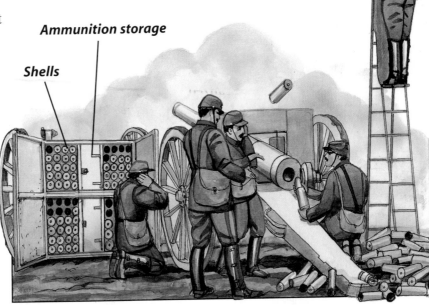

Fire-control observer

Steel shield protects observer

Ammunition storage

Shells

Trench Warfare

By 1915, a network of trenches stretched from the Belgian coast to Switzerland. Most trench systems — like the one shown here — had a front-line trench protected by rolls of barbed wire. Behind this were a support trench and then reserve trenches. They were connected to each other by communication trenches.

In an offensive, soldiers moved up to the front-line trenches. After an artillery bombardment, they went "over the top" (climbed out of their trenches) to attack the enemy. Casualties were generally very heavy because of the greater firepower of the defenders. Men often became entangled in barbed wire and were slaughtered by enemy machine-gun fire.

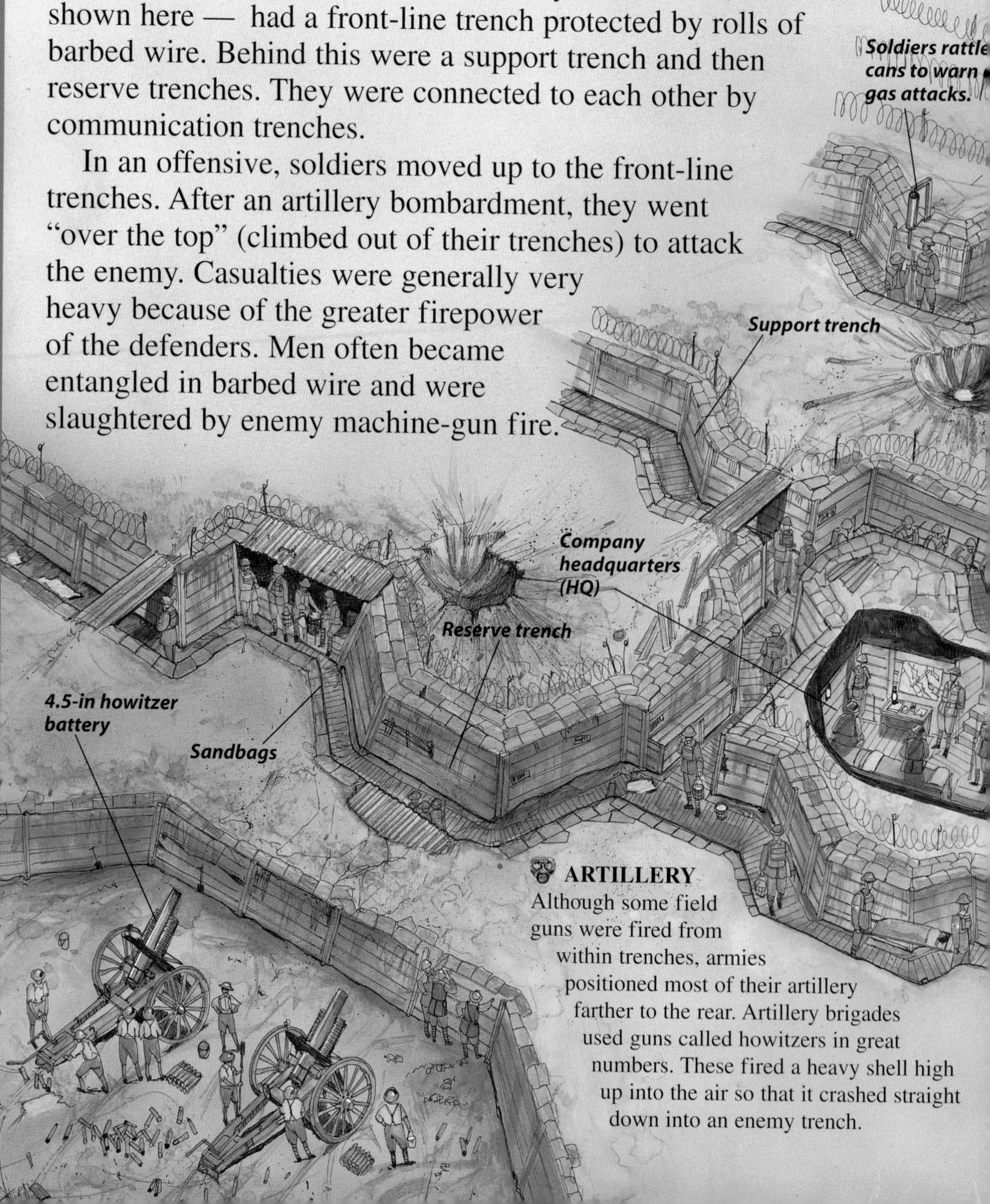

Soldiers rattle cans to warn gas attacks.

Support trench

Company headquarters (HQ)

Reserve trench

4.5-in howitzer battery

Sandbags

ARTILLERY

Although some field guns were fired from within trenches, armies positioned most of their artillery farther to the rear. Artillery brigades used guns called howitzers in great numbers. These fired a heavy shell high up into the air so that it crashed straight down into an enemy trench.

NO MAN'S LAND

Soldiers from each side faced each other across a strip of ground called No Man's Land, which in some places might be as wide as a mile but in others might be only 165 feet (50 meters) across. At night, patrols would be sent out to attack the enemy's defenses. It was dangerous work.

German trenches

No Man's Land

Barbed wire

Trench periscope

Front-line trench

Forward observation post

Light machine gun team

Trench-scaling ladders

Fire step

Communication trench

TRENCH EQUIPMENT

MACHINE GUNS

Machine guns, such as the British Vickers or the German Maxim, were one of the most deadly weapons on the Western Front. Operated by a two-man crew, the guns fired 400-500 bullets every minute.

British Vickers machine gun

GAS MASKS

Germany first used poison gas in 1915. Released from cylinders or fired from shells, gas killed men without protective masks. Gas masks were always very uncomfortable to wear.

PERISCOPES

Because it was dangerous to stick your head above the trench, troops in the front line used periscopes to look at the enemy trenches.

The mirror at the top of the periscope reflected the view to the observer below.

The Experience of War

Life in the trenches was usually grim. Apart from the dangers of enemy artillery and machine-gun fire, soldiers endured plagues of rats and lice. In wet weather the trenches became flooded.

Major offensives were rare, so for most of the time soldiers waited. They sent out patrols into No Man's Land, repaired damage, and watched for enemy activity. Soldiers worked mainly at night, as it was normally too dangerous for them to move around in daylight.

GENERALSHIP

The generals who commanded the armies of World War I have often been criticized because some people feel they did not care enough about their troops. Over the four years of war, millions of men were killed and wounded on the Western Front, but very little ground was won by either side.

In World War I, the side that could last longer won the war. In the end, the Allies were just too strong for the Central Powers.

French soldiers hang up their catch of rats.

TRENCH LIFE

Soldiers in the trenches often complained that boredom was their worst enemy. They tried to make life a little more fun. Rat-catching competitions were popular with troops on all sides.

Front-line soldiers developed their own special sense of humor, which helped them put up with hardships and the horrors of life in the front line. Keeping clean was also a constant problem in the trenches.

Most men became infected with lice, which lived in their clothes and caused diseases. Men spent hours trying to get rid of lice, whose bites were extremely irritating, but they always seemed to return.

Six German soldiers carry a wounded comrade.

🎭 MISERY IN THE MUD

Rain and artillery turned the battlefield into mud. Trenches collapsed; shell craters became big pools of slime where a man could drown in seconds. Moving supplies and guns became almost impossible, and it could take six to eight men to carry a stretcher, which would normally be carried by two soldiers.

A typical trench scene — muddy soldiers sheltering behind sandbags and barbed wire.

> "We heard screaming coming from a crater and there was a fellow up to his shoulders in mud. I said, 'Get your rifles and let him get hold of them.' But it was no use. The more we pulled and the more he struggled, the further he seemed to go down. And he died. There must have been thousands who died in the mud."
>
> — *An account written during the Battle of Passchendaele in 1917*

🎭 TRENCH RAIDS

As well as sending out patrols to repair defenses and scout for enemy activity, both sides carried out raids. Soldiers dashed across No Man's Land to destroy a section of enemy trench. Silence and surprise were vital.

Behind the Lines

Soldiers spent most of their time in the trenches or working just behind the front line, but they were allowed short periods of rest. Once they were away from the trenches, the men could wash — often for the first time in weeks — and have their uniforms cleaned. They could also eat hot, properly cooked food, and have time to get some uninterrupted sleep.

Army commanders knew that time and rest helped their troops recover from the ordeal of being in the front line, so they would be better prepared the next time they were sent into the trenches. Soldiers were encouraged to take part in sports and other activities.

CANTEENS
The canteen was a shop and café where troops could buy things from home, such as cigarettes, matches, and soft drinks, at reasonable prices.

WORK AND PLAY

MAINTENANCE
In the front line, weapons and other pieces of equipment could not be looked after properly. Time behind the lines gave soldiers a chance to mend and maintain equipment, ready for action again in the trenches.

MARKETS
Soldiers were usually paid when they came out of the line, and they liked to spend money on food and drink. They often bought local goods from Belgian or French civilians. This soldier is buying mistletoe for Christmas celebrations.

SPORT
To keep men fit and healthy, the army encouraged troops to take part in sports, and competitions between units were held. Among the more popular sports were soccer and boxing and, in cavalry regiments, horse racing.

MEDICAL SERVICES

In World War I, medical services were much better than in previous conflicts. Many more wounded men were saved from dying, so that large numbers of them needed long-term care.

A huge network of hospitals was set up behind the Western Front, and tens of thousands of nurses were recruited to look after the wounded. Soldiers with severe injuries had to be helped to come to terms with their wounds.

A nurse attends a soldier who has had his leg amputated (cut off).

ON WITH THE SHOW

Entertainment was a popular opportunity for men to forget about the horrors of trench warfare, if only for a short while.

Big stars were sometimes hired, but usually a unit provided its own amusement. Soldiers dressed up in silly costumes or in the style of famous entertainers of the day (left) and made fun of their officers.

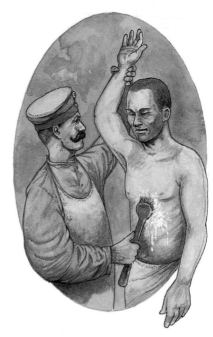

An attendant de-louses a soldier.

KEEPING CLEAN

After leaving the front line, soldiers marched to huge bath houses to get rid of the dirt and smell of the trenches. They left their clothes to be cleaned before washing themselves in large bath tubs holding up to fifty men.

When they had finished washing, they collected their newly cleaned uniforms. The men were checked to ensure that all lice had been killed, as lice could carry dangerous diseases such as cholera.

The Widening War

In 1915 the Allies, led by Britain, tried to invade and conquer the Turkish empire. However, they underestimated the fighting ability of the Turkish troops, and during 1915–16, the Allies were defeated at Gallipoli, Palestine, and Mesopotamia.

Toward the end of 1917, the British forces were reorganized and reinforced, and during the following year they repeatedly defeated the Turkish army. In October 1918, the Turks asked the Allies for peace terms.

"We could clearly see the Tommies charging across the flat [ground], under a perfect mass of bursting shells and shrapnel. The scrub with which the flat was covered caught fire, and I afterwards heard that many of the wounded, unable to escape, were burnt to death in it."

— Leonard Hart, a New Zealand soldier, on an attack by British soldiers (Tommies) at Gallipoli

Australian and New Zealand troops land at Anzac Cove, near Gallipoli, in 1915.

BEACH LANDINGS

In 1915, Allied troops landed at beaches around Gallipoli. They hoped to defeat the Turks and then march on the Turkish capital of Constantinople (modern Istanbul). The landings were a disaster. Allied troops were poorly led and equipped and were unable to push the Turks back. During the Gallipoli campaign, Australian and New Zealand troops also fought with great courage.

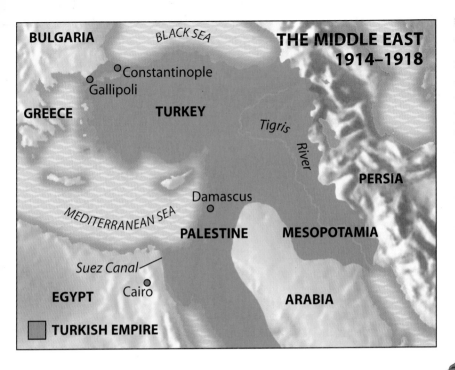

THE MIDDLE EAST
1914–1918

BULGARIA
BLACK SEA
Constantinople
Gallipoli
GREECE
TURKEY
Tigris
River
PERSIA
Damascus
MEDITERRANEAN SEA
PALESTINE
MESOPOTAMIA
Suez Canal
EGYPT
Cairo
ARABIA
☐ TURKISH EMPIRE

TURKISH TROOPS

Turkish infantry were highly respected by their Allied opponents because of their toughness. German officers helped train and equip the Turkish army. A German general, Liman von Sanders, played an important part in defeating the Allies at Gallipoli. The Turks fought with great determination until their final defeat in 1918.

THE TURKISH EMPIRE

In 1914, the Turkish empire included not only modern Turkey but also large areas of the Middle East. The British were afraid the Turks might invade Egypt and capture the Suez Canal, Britain's vital link with her colonies in the East.

To prevent this, the British invaded Palestine and, after many setbacks, captured the key city of Damascus in 1918. In Mesopotamia, the British eventually forced the Turks to retreat along the Tigris River. After the war, Turkey lost its empire.

T. E. Lawrence on a camel

A Turkish infantryman

LAWRENCE OF ARABIA

A British officer, Colonel T. E. Lawrence, was sent on a mission to help the Arab peoples fight the Turks, who then ruled over much of Arabia. Lawrence led the Arabs in a guerrilla war against the Turks in the desert.

Using camels and horses, the Arabs destroyed the main Turkish railway system in Arabia and captured the key port of Aqaba. Lawrence's leadership made him a legend.

Conflict in the East

Although the Russians suffered heavy losses fighting the Germans in 1914, they helped the western Allies (France and Britain) by drawing German troops away from the war on the Western Front. Russia scored more wins against the army of the Austro-Hungarian empire, which needed help from German troops in order to survive.

During 1915, the Germans began to force the Russians back into their own country. By 1917, the Russian army was at the point of collapse. In 1917, a revolution in Russia overthrew the czar (emperor), and the new government asked the Germans for a peace treaty. As a result, large areas of Russia came under German control.

Soldier of the Czech Legion

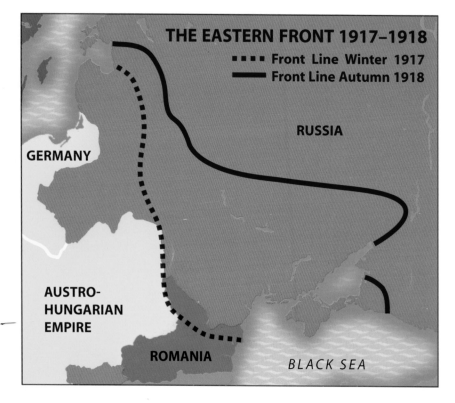

THE EASTERN FRONT 1917–1918

▪▪▪▪ **Front Line Winter 1917**
▬▬▬ **Front Line Autumn 1918**

GERMANY

RUSSIA

AUSTRO-HUNGARIAN EMPIRE

ROMANIA

BLACK SEA

🐾 AGAINST THE WAR

The Austro-Hungarian empire was made up of many nations, some of them opposed to the war. One of these was Czechoslovakia. Although Czechs were forced into the army, they were reluctant to fight the Russians. Czechs wanted independence, and the Czech Legion was set up to fight for an independent state.

🐾 WARFARE ON THE EASTERN FRONT

On the Western Front, fighting became bogged down in mud. In the east, warfare was more open, and armies marched long distances to fight.

The German army did most of the fighting against the Russians and defeated them on many occasions.

THE RUSSIAN ARMY

Russian soldiers fought with great bravery, often in terrible conditions, but they were poorly led and lacked the right weapons and equipment to take on the German army. Among the most elite Russian units was the proud Cossack cavalry.

During 1916, Allied weapons and equipment began to reach the Russian army, but this was too late to prevent the breakdown of the army in the following year.

A Russian Cossack cavalry trooper

THE CZAR

Czar Nicholas II, ruler of Russia, took over direct command of the army in 1915. He proved to be a poor commander-in-chief, however, and he eventually lost the respect of the army — and his own people.

After his overthrow in the revolution, he was imprisoned and killed in 1918.

The czar reviews his army (left).

THE REVOLUTION

In the spring of 1917, the Russian people were short of food and fed up with the war. They rose up against the czar and his government. A new government was set up in March, but in November 1917, the Bolsheviks seized power and asked for peace.

LENIN

Vladimir Ilyich Lenin was the chief Bolshevik leader. He promised Russians an end to the war and the right to run their own affairs. This made the Bolsheviks popular, especially among soldiers, whose support helped the Bolsheviks gain power. Once in power, the Bolsheviks set up a dictatorial state.

Bolshevik leader Vladimir Lenin

The War at Sea

$\mathbf{B}$ritain and Germany were the two main naval rivals. The British had a bigger fleet and imposed a naval blockade on Germany. This prevented ships from leaving or entering German ports. Apart from one attempt to break the blockade at the Battle of Jutland, the main German fleet stayed in port throughout the war.

Instead of taking on the British navy directly, the Germans attacked British merchant ships with U-boats (submarines). This strategy was very effective, and by early 1917, Britain was on the verge of starvation.

WARSHIPS

The modern battleship was the most important fighting ship of World War I. The first of these vessels was HMS *Dreadnought*, launched in 1906. This type of battleship was equipped with heavy guns in armored turrets. The most modern ships had 15-inch guns that could fire a shell up to 11 mi (18 km).

Dreadnoughts were protected by heavy steel armor, which made them hard to sink. Their powerful turbine engines gave them a fast top speed of up to 25 knots (28 mph).

HMS **Royal Oak** *fires its huge guns, which were housed in swivelling armored turrets.*

BATTLE OF JUTLAND

The Battle of Jutland was the one great naval engagement of the war. It was fought in the North Sea between May 31 and June 1, 1916. The Germans, commanded by Admiral Scheer, had hoped to trap part of the British fleet, but in the course of the battle the Germans were nearly caught by the more powerful British force. Realizing their danger, the Germans skillfully withdrew.

SEA WARFARE

DESTROYERS

The destroyer was a light and fast warship capable of speeds up to 30 knots (34 mph). A destroyer's main task was to attack larger ships with its torpedoes. It also used depth charges against submarines.

SUBMARINES

Armed with a gun and torpedoes, German U-boats sank more than 2,500 Allied vessels. The U-boats were eventually defeated by the Allies, who used anti-submarine warfare weapons such as depth charges and shepherded merchant ships into convoys (fleets) guarded by destroyers.

GERMAN COMMANDER

Admiral Reinhard Scheer became commander of the German High Seas Fleet in 1916 and led his forces into battle at Jutland. Although forced to retreat, Scheer claimed victory because the Germans had sunk a few more ships than the British.

🐵 THE *LUSITANIA*

The *Lusitania* was a British transatlantic liner that was sunk by a German U-boat off Ireland on May 7, 1915. Among the 1,198 people who drowned were 128 American citizens.

At the time, the United States was a neutral country, but the sinking of the *Lusitania* caused an outrage and turned the public opinion against Germany.

A contemporary picture of the Lusitania *incident conveys the horror of the sinking.*

LEST WE FORGET

The Sinking of the Lusitania. May 7th 1915

🐵 THE UNITED STATES ENTERS THE WAR

Germany's determination to starve Britain into submission using submarines also meant that many American ships trading with Britain were sunk. German leaders knew they were angering the United States, but they thought it was a risk worth taking. They were wrong. The United States declared war on Germany on April 6, 1917, and a powerful army was sent to France to help fight the Germans.

New Methods of Warfare

By the end of 1916, the armies of both sides on the Western Front were beginning to learn some of the lessons of trench warfare. They used new weapons and tactics to help troops cross No Man's Land. Among the weapons were new types of poison gas, light machine guns, mortars, and tanks. Soldiers were better trained; they fought in small groups that supported each other.

The most important change came in new ways of using artillery. Gunners perfected the "creeping barrage" so that as the infantry advanced, the artillery's fire "advanced" just ahead of them. More accurate guns fired special smoke shells to hide an infantry advance.

COMMUNICATIONS

The main way for a commander to keep in touch with his troops was by field telephone, but phone wires were often cut in an attack. As a result, soldiers and animals, such as homing pigeons and dogs, passed on messages.

TANKS

FAMOUS FIRST

The British army used tanks for the first time during the Battle of the Somme in September 1916. They were very unreliable and had a top road speed of just 3 mph (5 kph). By 1918, tanks had become more reliable and were more useful.

ARMORED MONSTER

The German army was not very impressed by tanks, and only built sixteen A7Vs. This mobile fortress had a crew of up to eighteen men and five machine guns. It was too awkward to be effective.

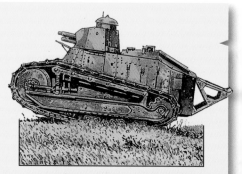

LIGHT AND EFFECTIVE

The Renault FT-17 light tank had a two-man crew and was armed with a machine gun or cannon. The FT-17 supported infantry attacks during the battles of 1918. It was popular with American troops.

A British tank attacks German front-line troops.

BATTLE OF CAMBRAI

The Battle of Cambrai, which began on November 20, 1917, was the first time that tanks led a major offensive.

The Germans were taken completely by surprise and were driven from their trenches, but within a couple of days most of the tanks had broken down or been destroyed by German artillery. The attack ground to a halt as the Germans rushed up reinforcements.

WAR UNDERGROUND

On the Western Front, mines were used by both sides. Troops dug long tunnels underneath the enemy trenches and packed them full of high explosives (below).

When the explosives were set off, they could totally destroy the enemy's front-line trench. If the enemy discovered a mine, they might dig a countermine in order to break into and destroy the original mine.

ARTIFICIAL TREES

To provide good observation positions, soldiers made artificial tree stumps from steel cylinders covered with wire mesh and canvas (above). Troops put these up at night next to a real tree stump, which would then be removed so that the enemy would think the false tree was real.

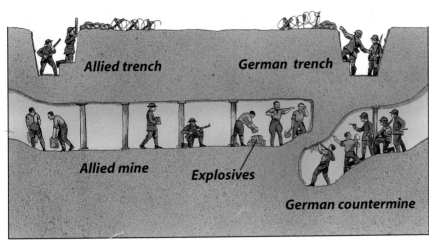

Allied trench

German trench

Allied mine

Explosives

German countermine

Battles in the Skies

The greatest advance in technology during the war came not on land or at sea, but in the air. Within four years, the rickety planes of 1914 had become effective war machines, which included fighter, reconnaissance, and bomber aircraft.

The size of air forces also grew enormously. In 1914, Britain went to war with about a hundred unarmed aircraft; by 1918, the newly formed Royal Air Force (RAF) had 22,000 aircraft of all types. Aviation was seen as a new and glamorous activity, and pilots became heroes.

A British Sopwith Camel chases a German Fokker triplane during an aerial dogfight.

🐵 THE ARMY'S EYES

The main function of an air force was reconnaissance — to see what the enemy was doing in and behind their front line.

In 1917, aircraft began to be fitted with simple radio sets so that observers could tell gunners where their shells were landing. Then the gunners could aim to hit the target.

🐵 DOGFIGHTS

At first aircraft were unarmed, but soon pilots began to carry pistols and rifles to shoot at each other. By 1915, machine guns were in use. The new fighter aircraft protected their own reconnaissance aircraft as well as shooting down enemy planes. By 1916, huge aerial battles, or "dogfights," were common. Pilots who had shot down five or more aircraft were known as aces. These included German Manfred von Richthofen (80 kills), Frenchman René Fonck (75 kills), and British pilot Edward "Mick" Mannock (73 kills).

AIRCRAFT

BRITAIN
The SE5a, one of the best British fighters of the war, was capable of taking on any German aircraft. The SE5a was armed with two machine guns and had a top speed of 125 mph (202 kph).

FRANCE AND THE UNITED STATES
The SPAD fighter was popular with both French and American pilots. The SPAD XIII was armed with two machine guns and had a top speed of 130 mph (210 kph).

GERMANY
Gotha bombers were used in raids on London and Paris. They carried up to 1,100 lb (500 kg) of bombs, although their slow maximum speed of 88 mph (142 kph) made them easy targets for Allied aircraft.

AIRSHIPS
Both the Allies and the Germans used airships during the war. Most German models were built by Count Zeppelin. These "zeppelins" used hydrogen gas to keep them in the air. Although not very fast, they could travel long distances — at least 620 miles (1,000 km) and back. They were mainly used for reconnaissance duties and to bomb cities in Britain and France. Zeppelins flew higher than most aircraft, and so were safe from attack. By 1917, however, improved fighter airplanes could fly higher and were thus able to shoot down the zeppelins.

German Zeppelin L-50

ALL-AMERICAN ACE
American Eddie Rickenbacker (above) was an automobile racer before the war, and it was only in March 1918 that he became a pilot. Despite his late start, Rickenbacker was a natural fighter pilot and soon began to build up a good score of kills. When the war ended he had shot down at least 26 enemy aircraft, making him the highest-scoring American pilot.

The Last Year of the War

By early 1918, the Allied blockade of German ports was causing great hardship, and people were beginning to starve. The arrival of American troops in France also meant that Allied troops greatly outnumbered the Germans. The German commanders then tried a desperate gamble to win the war.

The end of the war on the Eastern Front had freed German troops, and they were sent to the West to lead a last great offensive. Although the Germans did well at first, the Allied line held.

During the summer of 1918, the Allies went on the offensive and forced the German armies back. Realizing that the war was lost, the Germans agreed to peace talks on November 11, 1918.

An American infantryman, known as a "doughboy"

A British soldier takes a German prisoner.

🎭 THE UNITED STATES ARRIVES

When the United States declared war in April 1917, its army was small and not yet trained for modern warfare. After entering the war, the U.S. Army expanded rapidly. By November 1918, there were more than two million American soldiers in France.

🎭 GERMAN PRISONERS

During the great Allied offensive of 1918, German troops began to surrender in large numbers for the first time. The Allied forces were too strong, and many German soldiers were sick of the war. On a single day — September 29 — British troops captured more than 35,000 Germans.

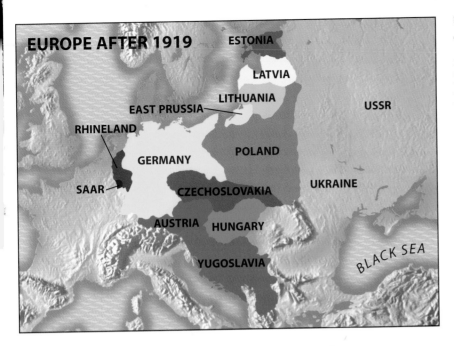

EUROPE AFTER 1919

ESTONIA
LATVIA
LITHUANIA
EAST PRUSSIA
USSR
RHINELAND
POLAND
GERMANY
SAAR
UKRAINE
CZECHOSLOVAKIA
AUSTRIA HUNGARY
YUGOSLAVIA
BLACK SEA

TREATY OF VERSAILLES

The 1919 Treaty of Versailles reorganized Europe, and as the losers of the war, the Central Powers suffered most. Germany lost lands to Poland and had to give up some of its territory to France. The Austro-Hungarian empire was broken up, and new states were put in its place, including the newly independent Czechoslovakia. In addition, the Baltic states of Lithuania, Latvia, and Estonia were created at the expense of Russia.

A MIXED CELEBRATION

In the Allied nations, the end of the war was greeted with wild enthusiasm, and people flocked into the streets to celebrate. In four years of fighting, however, over 13 million soldiers had been killed, and Europe had lost much of its wealth paying for the war. After 1918, the United States was confirmed as the world's most powerful industrial nation.

A French soldier returns home.

AN END TO THE FIGHTING

Once the Central Powers had accepted defeat, the great armies began to demobilize. Soldiers who had survived the war were now able to go home, but the process was slow — many men had to remain in the army until the end of 1919. This caused great bitterness.

"There was great liveliness, calls, cries, whistles and hooters sounding, noise and crowds. Great happiness prevailed. Every vehicle ... was boarded by people, most of whom waved flags."

— When news of the end of the war reached London, people crowded on to the streets to celebrate

Glossary

Turkish infantryman

Allies
The name given to the countries of France, Russia, Britain, and Belgium, who were allied together in their war against the Central Powers. The Allies were later joined by Italy and the United States.

Blockade
The policy adopted by the Allies to prevent ships carrying food and other goods from entering German ports.

Bolshevik
A member of the political party led by the Russian revolutionary Vladimir Lenin. It later became the Communist Party.

Central Powers
The nations of Germany, Austria-Hungary, and Turkey, which combined to fight the Allies.

Conscription
A military system in which young men are required to serve in the army or navy for about two years. In the event of war, the country can quickly call large numbers of men with military training back into the armed forces.

Demobilize
To reduce the size of a nation's armed forces by allowing servicemen to return to civilian life.

Depth charge
An underwater bomb used to blow up submarines.

Dictatorial state
A type of government in which the people have little or no say in how the country is run. The Bolsheviks replaced the dictatorial state of the czar with one of their own.

Dogfight
A battle fought in the air between two groups of opposing fighter aircraft.

Field gun
A light artillery weapon that fires shrapnel and explosives directly at enemy troops.

Guerrilla war
A type of war in which a small force uses surprise and deception to raid outposts and minor strong points. T. E. Lawrence helped lead an Arab force in a guerrilla war against the Turkish army in Arabia.

British Vickers machine gun

Howitzer

An artillery piece that lobs a shell containing explosives high into the air so that it comes down on the enemy. Howitzers were very effective in smashing trenches and dugouts.

Light machine gun

A machine gun that could be carried by a two-man crew. The British Lewis gun was an early example of a light machine gun.

Infantryman of the Czech legion

Merchant shipping

Civilian ships that carried cargoes of food and other goods from one country to another. Unlike naval ships, they did not usually carry any weapons, and they were very vulnerable to attacks by U-boats (submarines).

Mobilize

To make a country's armed forces ready for war. Civilians who had already trained as conscripts would be immediately called up to serve in the armed forces.

Mortar

A simple and lightweight piece of artillery used by the infantry. Similar to a miniature howitzer, a mortar shot a small shell up to a great height.

No Man's Land

The strip of ground that separated two opposing trench systems.

Reconnaissance

The way an army finds out about the position and movement of enemy forces. Aircraft play a major role in providing reconnaissance.

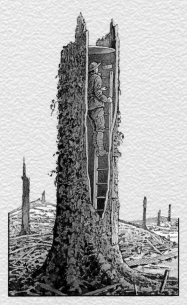

Lookout post

Revolution

The violent overthrow of a government or political system. The Russian Revolution of 1917 was one of the key events during World War I.

Torpedo

A long underwater missile fired from submarines and destroyers to sink enemy ships.

Western Front

The battleground in France and Belgium where Germany fought the Allies. It consisted of a line of trenches stretching from the Belgian coast to Switzerland.

INDEX